D0601974

Me and My World

Seasons

Sue Barraclough

WINDMILL
BOOKS

Published in 2009 in the United States by Windmill Books, LLC
303 Park Avenue South, Suite #1280, New York, NY 10010-3657

Design and typography: Natascha Frensch
Read Regular (European Community Design Registration 2008)
Read Regular and Read Xheavy copyright © Natascha Frensch 2001-2007

Publisher Cataloging Data

Barraclough, Sue
    Seasons / Sue Barraclough.
        p.   cm.—(Me and my world)
    Includes index.
    Summary: Simple text and photographs introduce the seasons, describing the
    weather of the different seasons and some of the changes in nature that occur.
    ISBN 978-1-60754-059-5 (library binding)
    ISBN 978-1-60754-066-3 (paperback)
    ISBN 978-1-60754-067-0 (6-pack)
1. Seasons—Juvenile literature   [1. Seasons   2. Vocabulary]   I. Title
II. Series
    508.2—dc22

Manufactured in China

Photo Credits: Cover © image100/Corbis; p 1,12 & 22 © Comstock/Corbis;
pp 2-3 © Dietrich Rose/zefa/Corbis; pp 4-5 Kathy Collins/Photographer's Choice/Getty;
pp 6-7 & 22 © Robert Llewellyn/zefa/Corbis; pp 8-9 © image100/Corbis; p 11 & 22 © Bloomimage/Corbis;
p13 & 22 Anne Ackerman/Taxi/Getty; p15 Ian Boddy, Science Photo Library; p16 Simon Wilkinson/Iconica/Getty;
p17 Superstudio/Taxi/Getty; pp 16-17 © Richard Hamilton Smith/Corbis; pp 20-21 © Craig Tuttle/Corbis

Contents

season

A **season** is a time of year.

spring

summer

Each season has different weather.

autumn

winter

5

spring

Spring is a season.

New green leaves and flowers grow.

summer

Summer is a season.

We play outside in warm weather.

sky

The sky is blue.

Butterflies fly from flower to flower in summer.

11

autumn

Autumn is a season.

Some leaves change color.

windy

Autumn is **windy**.

Windy weather is good for flying a kite.

13

leaves

In autumn, leaves fall.

This girl plays in the leaves.

winter

Winter is a season.

Many trees have no leaves.

cold

Winter is **cold**.

We wear warm clothes in winter.

snow

In winter, it can **snow**.

Playing in the snow is fun!

rainbow

We see **rainbows** in all seasons.

Sunshine and rain make a **rainbow** of many colors.

Picture Quiz Game

Can you find these things in the book?

kite

flowers

butterfly

leaves

What pages are they on?

Index Quiz Game

The index is on page 24.
Use the index to help you
answer these questions.

1. Which pages show **snow**?
   How many sleds can you count?

2. Which pages show summer is **warm**?
   How many children are playing?

3. Which pages show a **rainbow**?
   What two things make a rainbow?

4. Which page shows winter is **cold**?
   How many woolly hats can you see?

Index and Web Sites

Answers

Picture Quiz Game: The kite is on page 13. The flowers are on page 7. The butterfly is on page 11. The leaves are on page 12.
Index Quiz Game: 1. Page 18-19, three; 2. Page 9-10, three; 3. Page 20-21, sun and rain; 4. Page 17, one.

Web Sites
To ensure the currency and safety of recommended Internet links, Windmill maintains and updates an online list of sites related to the subject of this book. To access this list of We sites, please go to www.windmillbooks.com/weblinks and select this book's title.

For more great fiction and nonfiction, go to windmillbooks.com.